# THE
# DIFFICULT
# WHEEL

# THE DIFFICULT WHEEL

*Poems by*

## BETTY ADCOCK

Louisiana State University Press

Baton Rouge and London

1995

Designer: Melanie O'Quinn Samaha
Typeface: Bembo
Typesetter: Impressions, a division of Edwards Brothers, Inc.
Printer and binder: Thomson-Shore, Inc.


LIBRARY OF CONGRESS CATALOGING-IN-PUBLICATION DATA

Adcock, Betty.
    The difficult wheel : poems / by Betty Adcock.
        p.   cm.
    ISBN 0-8071-2022-7 (cl : alk. paper). — ISBN 0-8071-2023-5 (pbk. :
alk. paper)
    I. Title.
PS3551.D396D5   1995
811'.54—dc20                                             95-22420
                                                        CIP

The author offers grateful acknowledgment to the editors of the following periodicals, in which poems in this volume first appeared, some in slightly different form: *American Literary Review*, "East Texas Autumn as a Way to See Time"; *Georgia Review*, "Time After Time," "Valentine at Fifty"; *Kentucky Poetry Review*, "Prophecy"; *Negative Capability*, "Her Dying as a Bird: Small Fantasy for a Beloved Aunt"; *Pembroke Magazine*, "Living for a While in the Country"; *Shenandoah*, "After Geology, After Biology," "At the Age When You Get Bad News," "The Mind," "Threshold," "To a Young Feminist Who Wants to Be Free," "The Woman Hidden in This Painting," "Writing Poems Late"; *Southern Humanities Review*, "The Bird Woman"; *Southern Poetry Review*, "Illuminations," "New South"; *Southern Review*, " 'In Another Life . . . ,' " "Lines to a Past Love," "The Mad Widow: The Widow Speaking," "White Rhinoceros"; *Tar River Poetry*, "One of a Kind," "Poem for Dizzy," "Time at the Movies," "Voyages." "Four from the Spider" first appeared in *The Gettysburg Review*, Vol. 5, No. 4, and is reprinted here by permission of the editors. "Written at a Country Mansion of the 1920s, Now Partially Restored as a Writing Retreat for Poets" appeared in *Weymouth: An Anthology of Poetry* (St. Andrews Press, 1987).

*for Scott Byrd*

*1935–1995*

*rare and careful reader, friend to poetry and poets*

*Despite the times, the cursed spite*
*there is still music*
*in the leaves and magic in the cunning*
*spiral of a snail, and falling water*
*with its lovely, ruinous cascade of sound,*
*all this that beggars speech and yet*
*gives tongue.*

—Eleanor Wilner

# CONTENTS

## I

## II

# III

I

# PROPHECY

*with a borrowing from Stevie Smith*

The poets have gone out looking for God again,
having no choice,
disguising as typeface, mirror, theory's fretful counterturn
the old search in the voice.

The trees still wave, green as a summer sea.
The grain still makes in the ear
a richness we can almost hear.
And the world still comes to be. And not to be.

*Nothing has changed, really,* we whisper,
though all we trumpet is the changing stir.
And the air is emptied where they were:
spirits, gods, demons, with whatever

named them gone like fallen wind.
Did we imagine they had wings?
Perhaps they thought they did,
until we learned and flew ourselves, singing.

They went out the way stars do, slowly,
the long centuries of flight
unspiraling from them. They melted quite
like Icarus or those figures of ordinary

murderers and monarchs remade in wax museums.
Like these, they lack all metaphor
to tell what they were for.
And we lack any means to . . . any means.

What we do have is light. See how they are still burning—
all those classical noses, Coyote's laughing muzzle,

Shiva's raised foot, Christ's cheek, the dazzle
of leafy-armed women darkening, ashy-turning.

With this candle to see by, the poets are calling
and calling, much further out than they thought,
not kneeling but falling.

# ONE OF A KIND

. . . the mule is offspring of an ass
and a mare, combining the strength of
the horse with the endurance of the
ass. It is incapable of procreation.
        —dictionary definition

Consider the mule, thick as a stump,
clay-flecked and ugly in any of several
dismal colors. His knobbled bones hold up
neither one true kind nor the other.

Made like a conjecture,
he stands in his singular inch
of time, the present tense
he runs in order to perish of it.
Over and over, he dies out.

No wide-flung history of *horse* can race
in his stalled sleep, no wind's long-running story.
The future will foal through him no trace
of the delicate-paced small ass of the sand
or the heavy wild hoof of Mongolia

to say the blood and earth continuous.
I think even the utterly domestic
dray and donkey remember in their dreaming flesh
all that it matters to remember:
America's tall grass wandering unfenced,
Spain chinked with cobbles, Arabia breasting
the desert. And how the little streets of Jerusalem
were lit blue with evening,
winding like veins toward the heart.

Not this one. Born canceled, he works and balks,
angry always in the muscle of his unknowing,
himself his only tribe, and that one going.
He waits in his rubbly coat for dark,

rowing and rowing the stony field,
turning the difficult wheel.

He bears hard goods of this world on his back,
and the black whip and the man who wields the whip—
the man who is angry too, sensing the serious kinship.

# THE MIND

*after Dr. Oliver Sacks*

It's nothing you can put your finger on:
a box of matches scatters on the floor;
autistic twin savants can name the number,
each exactly half, and add the sum
in a single instant. Asked how they do it,
they reply in unison. *We see. We see it.*

We can't be sure of where, in time, we'll be:
this man can't get past nineteen forty-three.
He remembers all up to that year, not one
day later than his own age twenty-four.
Each morning he confronts old age and terror
fresh in his mirror, then hides in the garden.

You could wake up where nothing is the same:
a man of great intelligence has learned
to lose the use of objects and the name
of almost everything: hat, glove, the stern
face of his uncomprehending wife
who joins his world in being new for life.

It's nothing you can put your finger on:
but aren't we all as wise, unwise, or passing strange
as these? We're closets full of snowshoes in July,
years and ghosts for which we've lost all name
though our lists and cries fill up the world with language.
We build a craft of air and glue and balsa,
load it with flammable numbers, that hat, a glove,
then layer on the shiny colored gloss,
add torch songs, our younger faces, murder, love.

Thus compassless and dangerous,
good at belief and good at lies,
we say together: *Yes, we see it.*
And it flies.

7

# ARGUMENT

There's no real difference between
a spear and a nuclear rocket. Both
are just technology, and I shouldn't
like being killed by a spear any
more than by an intercontinental
missile. What I'm saying is, a
death's a death; it comes to the
same thing.
                    —the Younger Poet at dinner


I can't deny you know much more
about some worlds than I can know.
You've studied physics.
Your poems are exquisite with learning.

And I hadn't thought I'd been here long enough
to be some part of an older generation,
having no wisdom but only a skulking
certainty that might actually be furred—

or not far from it. Something truly old
rises in me at what you've said,
something like smoke and a shadow unfolding
at the edge of an interior fire.

How to answer, young friend,
your sure equation? A spear
is attached to a specific hand and eye
until the last fraction of a minute:

my argument's in that,
and in the skill of the individual
who determines the whole of this act,
including the audible cracking of bone,

the breath going out, the screech
a soul makes leaving—

that bubble and prayer of death
immediate, tangible as the self.

Let's say it's almost a kind of justice
that the man who releases a spear
must watch the death he's made, if only
to retrieve the bloody spear.

This is not pleasant conversation,
but no one is talking about pleasure.
We are talking about man. A man.
A man who has thrown with utmost care

a spear. He has real blood on him;
even a gun will take away such obligation.
But this act is local and stays local
as when a wooden plow is used, an ax, an awl.

The definers say a plow's as much technology
as a computer is, meaning whatever works
in human hands. Whatever works.
But there is a dividing line not named

by the namers, a line glare-blue, drawn
by no hand we can remember, clear
as a cave painting in firelight.
Something like *bear*

stands up between the rocket and the spear.

# AFTER GEOLOGY,
# AFTER BIOLOGY

In school we learned how continental plates
slipped, drifting in monumental sleep
across the face of possibility;
how the land unshaped itself,
reshaping insubstantialities
hard toward another life, always
another life, disjunct and continuous.

In their own slow parallel, the animals
grew unfamiliar to each other,
altering their shadows
with new sizes or limbs or noses,
necessity's estrangements into change.

Remember how we couldn't quite believe it,
sitting under the eyes of Mr. Saunders
who wasn't sure he, a Baptist, believed it either?
And, if believing, we couldn't exactly think
that grand and ponderous meander
behind us like unwound, unseeable film
all the way to black.

Think now. The ordinary little past of anyone
has sped colliding
with some other hemisphere entirely,
and at velocities that make one lifetime
all a motion sickness, an agitation
of disappearances.

What new bone can
invent itself where distance dies
and time no longer separates?
What migration gathers miles in us
toward utter absence?
Might we ask back our drowsy obsolete

saunter into future?  One more chance
at the old, procrastinating, any-which-way dance?

No.  Never.  It's enough to make you say,
with Mr. Saunders after class,
*Now let us pray.*

# To a Young Feminist Who Wants to Be Free

You describe your grandmothers walking straight
off the boats from Finland, Latvia
too late, early in this century, to bear blame
for sins we're bound to expiate:
*in their funny hats, a potato in each pocket,*
*what possible American shame*
*could they hand down to me?* You have your own
angers, you say. So much for the nineteenth
century's slavery, lynchings, native massacre, and the teeth
of cities still gnawing off the feet of survivors,
those gigantic traps still set.
You blame the men and free yourself of time
and fathers, displaced from more
than countries lost. Or never claimed.

I can't help thinking of the miserably hot summer
I taught in Michigan, where a July Fourth
was the whole *treasury of virtue* hammered home
in speeches praising Michigan and the lever of the war
that undid slavery and joined the union back.
Yet that whole campus was the record of a severing:
not one face in any class was black.
And only a few miles distant, our Detroit
was roiling and afire.
The students laughed at my slow southern accent,
joked that I'd brought the unaccustomed heat.

Perhaps I know too much, living as I must
with the lives (in letters) of great- and twice-great-
grandmothers,
southern women talking about their slaves
as if it were ordinary. It was. Sometimes the wills are there:
whole black families listed with the mules. It's terrible enough
to die about, and people did: the saviors and the guilty

and the simple poor.  Never believe it's gone.
The stain is mine and I can't pass it anywhere but on,
and to my own.  I live with what the past will not stop
proffering.  I think it makes me wiser than you are,
who measure by the careful inch your accident
of time here and your innocence.

It lets you be only the victim,
lets you find the gold-
eyed goat still waiting in the bushes
to be bled.

Anyone who came here anytime
came here to take this country's gifts.
Not even you may refuse this one:
what's built on darkness rests on it.
And there is wisdom yet, though hard to see
in this peculiar light.  It is the only light
we've got.  And when was it *not* the case
(except in hell) that land and history
wear another's face?
Here is the necessary, fearsome, precious,
backward whole embrace.

# THRESHOLD

They are brittle, tucked carefully as saved letters
into the envelopes of their heavy coats.
You've seen them in the park
they think might be the bad forest
in the storyteller's heart.
Holding up faces pained as newborns',
they seem likewise never to have meant
to reach their destinations.

You've seen how they move, the lame
halting, the halt on the tortuous lam.
Partly it's the body's faulty music
and partly a dodge, a circumvention
of rhythms they no longer want to keep.
This tedious stealth is more than fear
of being mugged, of falling or running out
of breath that laps too shallow at their ribs.

They are slowed by newer wounds: this April
sharpening its countless blades, too green.
Too green the new leaves. Too red the burst
run-over squirrel and the gang of tulips on the hill,
extortionists. See the shawled old women wince
at heated pinks azaleas proffer, at goldfinches
alight, and morning-brightened gutter water.

Even the white hillocks of an old man's own
knuckles in the sun will seem too much.
Things will not dim. No matter how the eye
squints out the day's blue fires,
the dogwood in the wind's a riot
of shooting stars.

And this accounts for cataracts, for deafness
feigned or real, for the narcotic ache
and lost recall, for the retreat
into a sepia past, into the simpler

terror of the prowler and the maniac.
Hope will keep the body and its soul
indoors, content with the equivalents
of hotplates and thin, discolored cats.

Though all the shades drawn down will not
narrow the light one whit, nor stay
the hundred burning tongues of forsythia.
The tighter the bolt, the wider open
our one embrace is flung
from flesh to the wild, marauding garden.

# TIME AFTER TIME

An Australian sound engineer has
developed a unique way of clearing
the hiss and clatter out of vintage
jazz recordings.
—Associated Press


Time: it does things
out there among the galaxies.
Clatter and hiss?  Perhaps.
That's one metaphor for distance

which is time.  And our remembering?
There's less and less,
the dissonance of *now* and *then*
no longer audible when
mechanics cancels difference.

So out with the scritch of decades,
the sizzle and scar of error,
remembrance's waver, susurrus
of mortality, dust-riff, and blues-ether.

We will turn *them* into *us,*
our sound loud as a spotlight,
bright as an electronic toy,
cleansed of those troublesome sixty years
and that old distortion: joy.

# LINES TO A PAST LOVE

These are dead: the otter
of our thaws, the later and dangerous
badger, the arboreal cat
in the snowy branches of silence.
Even the soul's mouse, hesitant
with its stanzas of footprints,
is a scatter of transparent bones.
The hawk flies with bleeding stumps,
looks for her talons.

Where these lived redly in the heart,
wrestled in cave and passage,
or drank through my dreaming fingers,
only ghosts are, keeping in darkness
though the world brings news:

a seal hunt is raging;
the condor's egg is a tomb;
caribou die of strange lichens.
I think of the poisonous reasons
and I remember you.

I've slipped out of those pelts,
out of the wings and their wind.
I fold away meadows and forests.
On my knees by a circle of stones
I've opened a different map.
Snake in a new skin, unaccountable lizard,
toad in a niche of winter, spirit me.
I'm about to start over, a fish-eyed thing,
too old to love, too ignorant to sing.

# WHITE RHINOCEROS

Immense, stuck with two nose-horns, they're ghostly
cousins of the unicorn's first draft,
though that is hard to credit. Two sit,
two stand in the sand trucked in
to make a plain. It's African
terrain as Carolina U.S.A. imagines it.
Complete with lifelike boulders of concrete.

Not really white, all four have rolled the sand
into a final skin. We'll wait all morning
for the largest one to move
not much, the great head a kind of engine
pulling the body like a Macy's giant balloon.
It's said they're fast. Perhaps that's just momentum.
Any serious motion they began
would have to last, and increase.
But we won't see them run.
In this world that's found them,
they cannot have begun,
not for our money or their own
lost currencies of rut and territory.

When one lies down, the shape's a complication.
No place to put the huge, pulled-taffy face.
A vasty nostril's squashed, the lip's displaced.
No place to put a horizontal half-ton leg and foot.
Bone, flesh slab, and leather undertake
a cosmic squirm, a quake
for antique comfort's sake.

How life has yearned all ways for more of itself!

We think the rhinos dream. We think that
the same way we guessed from a distance
they might be fiberglass. Closer,
we saw two bump like dreamy train cars,
their eyes not looking anywhere

but looking nonetheless.
We think they listen. The small ears twitch
as if they listen.
What image comes to them, what voice?
Some surreal version
of *Lost World* from late-night television?
Or can they imagine only this blurred
landscape of made indecision,
this air drilled with Carolina birds?

Perhaps the others gone or nearly missing
sing to these? Perhaps the Aurochs
sings four hundred years of darkness,
prototype of all our cattle, bull
that held Europa. And does the Quagga,
onomatopoeic, cry out the name
heard by the Hottentots who gave it back?
Perhaps the Blue Buck answers reverie
in our rhinos who now are nearly myth
themselves, who may be humming as the Tiger hums
far under consciousness, a vanishing.
If the discarded continents, snowy with ghosts,
make such a music—if
behind the forehead's massive boneplate
the rhinos know that shadow descant ringing—
we do not think *for us.*
We think *the fey*
*rhinoceros.*
        We think that.

# FOUR FROM THE SPIDER

Enact yourself between fixed points,
but loosely—let the wind anoint
clarity with death, and death with light.
Live on the sheerest opposites.

Dance in a thin but working order.
Choreograph a net that severs
with just such difficulty as
makes it worth the making-over.

Take what comes, food or the random blown,
with indiscriminate self outspun.
The world is everything that sticks.
Choose. Then count illusion's tricks.

In the season's final filament be caught.
Nothing—not saving grace nor closing argument—
attaches to your having been
the wheel you turned in.

II

# STRAYING INTO
# FEBRUARY WOODS

A few things seem to stay. Beeches
have kept their pale brown leaves
all winter. Now the wind moves them,
full-skirted dancers on a hill of skeletons.
Lying still on the next slope, I grow fond
of these distances, of the stark
one-syllabled rocks and sticks,
even the ones that poke me in the back,
reminders. I like drifting in these temperatures,
a time traveler who's lost her summer picnic.

I'm getting old, older anyway
than I'm used to thinking of.
Would my friends like this winter afternoon,
all sun because the barriers are down,
each leaf-creak or insect an event?
I doubt it. My friends like noise and love.

But here I don't mind doubting anything.
Or guessing wild. Imagine all that goes
when summer goes: all that living *stuff.*
Doesn't it reject us by coming back?
Wasp thrum, birdsong, the jagged best
arias of the creek—all die with autumn's fortune,
and are yet next summer so exactly present
no note is ever lost. Nothing in us
can do that. With the generations,
we always lose the tunes.

Keats said it better far.

What I hear now is poetry,
that next to nothing. I'm here
simply to hear such shading

slight and equal to the coming night.
I claim the forest privilege
of talking out loud to myself . . .

just as last August, at high summer buzz and swelter,
and to come next August, the voices of this hillside
repeated, will repeat
everything, perhaps even a woman speaking,
with only the greenest lover's
*forever    forever    forever.*

# THE WOMAN HIDDEN
# IN THIS PAINTING

Like a renegade summer she begins
to burn outside defining lines
almost as if a child's hand traced
and lost her.
Window, leaf, bird, the stony hill
absorb her until the body's only
a put-off dress, a color vanishing
so slowly the watcher in his trance
misses it entirely.

Now a lifting as if her arms are lifting,
a soaring sheer
stretch—and her skin is air.
Or say a string of beads has scattered
and the whole light gathers them
invisible in bright haze
as the pear that might have rested
where morning struck such shine from the table.

One rose gray feather on the sill
implies the silk-on-silk of dove call
she might hear. Just there,
the open curtain would brush her fingers
and the plain white cup obscure
her wrist unbraceleted.

One line might draw her back, a traveler again
in flesh upon a track of bone,
to cast against the sun-drenched wall
a shadow, dark heel knit to her heel,
time plangent in the bell-bright blue
shawl on her shoulder. See
how she was and will be here,
a dream staining the light the painter
has forgotten?

Beyond, beyond the half-open curtain,
the apron of grass is, and ribboning
paths hemstitched with chicory.
Farther still (O the eye is endless)
dark trees feather a restless sky.
She will return in this, a mist
at her throat, her arms reddened
with horizon. The gray of the hare's flank
is the gray her eyes give back.

And pale. The face when we have seen it
will be pale beneath the glow
the wind's pearls told her.
*Presence,* she whispers,
a changing
chink of weather in the window.

# "In Another Life . . ."

People will say it at parties, speaking of the shock
one feels at being quite familiar with some place one's never been,
or with a face not seen before.  Again
last night I heard it from a friend just home
from the south of France.  And years ago I knew a man
who'd say it meaning something else entirely.  He'd bring
whole strings of former incarnations in to dinner.

But those chronologies are wrong.
The other life exists, if it exists, alongside this one.
If there were maps for such strange latitudes
they'd read: *unchosen parallel.*

In mine, these hands learned calm and gardening,
the catch of fabric against a roughened palm,
the steam of canning kettles, jelly making.
In the lifeline of that shadow–hand, I stayed.
Say I married a man from the county.  He sells insurance
in the town.  Really just a farm boy
who lucked into another living
because it was the 1950s and you could.
Still, our garden is the biggest one around.

We have children, grown now and ordinary as potatoes.
They didn't really know how to surprise us.
We had plain troubles, hard but workable.
One son went into business with his dad.
I think I teach at the high school
the way my mother did
before the path approaching me divided.
The old poems make me oddly happy.

And my father spent his age with us, died easy
one cold late November.  In his sleep.

We kept the house I was born in,
rambling big rooms, the ways the dead stay on

in the scents of fireplaces and old furniture,
a worn feel to all the corners.
Like everyone, we sold the big acreage,
saving the pecan orchard, the peaches.
And we kept the life, somewhat: our garden,
a few horses, and a goat.

But some days, maybe in the middle of church
when Presbyterian voices
drag those hymns as if for bodies,
or in the middle of a class of seniors, or a row
of beans or stitches, papers to grade,
grandchildren, or petunias, I'll feel a shade
creep over me, a loneliness
so deep and strange it is like travel
without hope of home. And I'm overcome
with a wish so strong I jump,
thinking I've spoken.
Then, like the women in those harvest paintings,
I am *woman with a basket,* eyes distracted,
face turning away. And the basket overflowing,
and all the landscape golden and bereft.

That's when I reach toward what is not
there, this woman in the shut room of a city
who writes with a wall of books behind her,
writes this reaching toward the woman who is not
here, whose strong hands drop as she stops work to lose
all touch, standing in the yard in wonder at such sadness
that she never did see Greece or take the time
to think the way she knew she could, or write things down.
She had meant to do that, meant to write.
Oh what was it she had meant to write?

Now two women wake. Let's say they do.
Or one wakes and one cannot,
but which is not yet known. Two wake
in places that may or may not be real.
Their hands are warm and different and still.
They're blinking, startled as two children.
Neither can imagine where the daydream

came from, how it so absorbed her
it might have been
a depth-charged sleeping dream,
the kind you live in every muscle before dawn.

# REVENANT

Horizontal in my green coat,
resting my head on a log, I must have seemed
some part of autumn that refused to turn,
under the flicker's scissoring and the squirrel's
scribble against an iron sky.

And this is a simple story. Let loose
it will run by itself to the place
where blanched sun laced through near-bare branches
and the day seemed to pour from the hawk's gyre.

To doze in woods is to rest on the hard edge
of fear, so you're awake
to what you can neither see nor dream
nor come at with a name.
And yet I thought at first of hikers
in that crash of leaves, a sound that dimmed
at the edges then came back all wrong
because there was no order in it,
no human rhythm.

I did not quite cry out but froze the moment
I saw him see me, saw the heavy-antlered head
alter its slant.
He moved in the slow way animals will seem
to move in children's picture books,
on each page larger, clearer—
until he was so close I saw the shine
on raised black nostrils,
and I thought stupidly of creeks,
how they go black with mystery
underneath the winter's lens of ice.

Browsing the leaf-quilted floor, huffing,
the deer edged closer, stopped, his eyes on mine;
and the moment went sly as a dream, the world

unhinged a little, light with reckoning and change.
But there was no change, no revelation.  None.
No help for the poet's old protean
longing to become, to be undone.

Whole minutes—two? three? A look, a tangle
of otherness tight as bramble, odd
as a long fall.  Nothing
had ever happened or ever would
while I could hear that stranger-breath and see
each separate shoulder hair shift color as he blew
a snort like a horse's.  How exact the hoof's design
on fallen leaves, lifting and setting down
with such small sound I might be still alone.

And someone now is saying this is one of those
dense and symbol-laden moments poets make
to force and tease, the whole thing false
with sexual curvature and hidden weight.
This could be the father coming back
in the form he killed.  Or the father's
nemesis.  Or it could be a sweet communion,
that old lie.

Finally huge and motionless as a tree
and nearer than my senses wished to know,
he took on, like a cloak, the simple dusk.
And if that looks like poetry, like loss,
the shadow of loss, or memory like black water
on his sides, then let it be
these words as good as any.
                              He leapt straight up
as if to lose that covering thought.
He turned and caught
the barest gilding of last light
and stirred the leaves to sharp explosion
and was gone. A distant brushy rustle.

It took me longer to begin to leave.
Some tears shook from me without regret or reason,
a kind of backward praise.  For what,
I neither know nor quite forget.

# VOYAGES

We were five girls prowling alleyways behind the houses,
having skipped math class for any and no reason.
Equipped with too many camelhair coats, too many cashmeres,
we were privileged and sure and dumb, isolated
without knowing it, smug in our small crime, playing
hooky from Miss Hockaday's Boarding School for young ladies.
Looking for anything that wouldn't be boring
as we defined that, we'd gone off exploring the going-downhill
neighborhoods around our tight Victorian schoolgrounds.
The houses were fronted with concrete porches,
venetian blinds drawn tight against the sun.

Somebody had told us an eccentric lived where one
back fence got strangely high and something stuck over
the top. We didn't care what it was, but we went anyway,
giggling with hope for the freakish: bodies stashed and decaying,
a madwoman pulling her hair, maybe a maniac in a cage.
Anything sufficiently awful would have done.

But when we came close enough to look through
the inch of space between two badly placed fenceboards,
we saw only the ordinary, grown grotesque and huge:
somebody was building a sailboat bigger than most city backyards,
bigger almost than the house it belonged to,
mast towering high in a brass-and-blue afternoon.
This was in the middle of Dallas, Texas—
the middle of the 1950s, which had us
(though we didn't yet know this) by the throat.
Here was a backyard entirely full of boat,
out of scale, out of the Bible, maybe out of a movie,
all rescue and ornament. It looked to be something between
a galleon and a Viking ship, larger than we could imagine
in such a space, with sails and riggings and a face on the prow
(about which we made much but which neither smiled nor frowned).

Gasping, overplaying the scene, we guessed at the kind
of old fool who would give a lifetime to building this thing.
Then one of us asked for a light for a cigarette
and we all knew how easy it would be to swipe
a newspaper, light it, and toss it onto the deck
of that great wooden landlocked ark, watch it go up.

But of course we didn't do it and nobody of course came out
of that house and we of course went back
in time for English and to sneak out of P.E. later
for hamburgers at Mitch's where the blue-collar boys
leaned in their ducktails against the bar.

But before we did that, we stood for a while clumped
and smoking, pushed into silence by palpable obsession
where it sat as if it belonged on parched Dallas grass,
a stunned, unfinished restlessness.

And didn't the ground just then, under our penny-
loafers, give the tiniest heave?  Didn't we feel how thin
the grass was, like a coat of light paint, like green ice
over something unmanageable?  How thin the sun
became for a minute, the rest of our future dimming
and wavy and vast, even tomorrow's pop quiz and softball practice—

as if all around us were depths we really could drown in.

# THE MAD WIDOW:
# TWO POEMS

## THE WIDOW SEEN

All over the neighborhood, the sun
is spilling through October.
Days like stained glass take the light
for utter change—
as Emma does, who has sat all summer
in her silent, darkened house.
This time of year she ranges tirelessly
between front doorstep and the street,
pacing a drama only she can read,
busy as a caged mouse on a wheel.

She seems to come out only for the carillon
of color in the maple tree,
for the trilling dogwood and the tolling oak.
Disoriented sentry, she practices a sullen
back and forth and mutter, some incantation
we can't quite hear as we pass by with dogs
on leashes, or running in our orange or lime
or peach-bright polyesters.

Each time she reaches her front door she bangs it shut
so hard and so often in succession,
the cats take fright all down the block
and people on other streets look up
from what they're doing to say, *What is that noise?*
What does Emma teach us of effect and cause?

A rage brings down the world again:
the brilliant windows of the light,
the colors and the bells undone.
She stands in rubble she can keep.
Beside her splintering door to winter,
life goes all to pieces at her feet.

## THE WIDOW SPEAKING

Morning comes in on strings of light,
the empty white bodies of dream
flapping noiselessly, the years scrubbed
and nameless as garments at a yard sale.

I know about the coffee cups:
it matters which one I choose. Everything matters.
I can take an hour just deciding. Every day
sends in its light until I pull it down,
tumbling the whole thing, poles broken
sheets of sunlight and white cloud-shirts collapsing.

My children sang of sunbeams, school songs,
Sunday school. Mornings were red with cardinals.
We fed them, even tamed one once. They're gone.
My son is dark and large. My daughter's
married. My life's what I remember a long time:
how I woke and he was dead beside me.
Years I had wished him off me, prayed to lose
his whiskey, his threats, the gun he'd wave empty.

Why then did my life break with his stroke?
Fifty is too old. Too old to have a wish
made flesh, cold flesh white as plaster of paris.
The cost of that's the secret
no one knows I hold
as if it were a child of my old age.
I *am* like Sarah in the Bible, granted late
what I most wanted. But it's a child born crooked,
immaterial, full of particular requirements.

There's so much to remember: how to walk
beneath the autumn trees, and what to say,
and how hard to shut the door to kill the evil
that crouches on the doorsill like a cripple.
Or is it just a child, its face my own
before I grew into this marriage?
I don't know. I know I have to choose.
*Remember the cup* is what I hear,

like something from church.
Every morning I pour the made dark in.
—Today this blue one
threaded with deep cracks around the rim?

# POEM FOR DIZZY

written after discovering that
no poem in *The Anthology of Jazz
Poetry* is written to, for, or about
Dizzy Gillespie, who was cocreator
(with Charlie Parker) of bebop,
the style that ushered in the modern
jazz era


Sweet and sly, you were all business when the old bent-
skyward horn went up. Sometimes it went up like a rocket,
sometimes like a gentle-turning lark
high on a summer day. It could blow an island wind
snapping a line of red and yellow clothes
hard against blue.
The breath pouring into that banged-up
brass inclination heavenward
gave us lesson number one: *Be.*
Lesson number two came naturally.

And you were serious as sunrise. Those who scoffed
or bristled at the little stageside dance,
the cutting-up, the jokes and jive, have all gone off
to other targets. And you, Dizzy,
you've gone off too, asleep in your chair,
leaving us bereft. There was nobody better.

But there were lives the poets would want more—
for tragedy or politics, harsher
experiments: Bird's drugged vortex into *gone,*
Coltrane's absolute, Monk's edgy monologues, the demon
Miles Davis posed as, then became.
But you played clown, put everybody on.
You played the house, but played a soul into the horn.
And you outlived them all. This too was real jazz.

Talking, you were evasive, slant as a riff
around a melody, more private maybe

than anybody knew.  I remember your one week
in our town, 1970:
afternoons you'd wander with your camera.
Putting his flute back in its case, Moody told us:
*He does that every place we go, walks around*
*for hours by himself, just taking pictures*
*of wherever it is he is.*  Lesson number one.

You looked like the face of South Wind
in my childhood picture book,
like the best cherub
Italy ever chiseled above a doge
or saint, rich man, or pope.
What were you storing in those blown-out cheeks
all the years?  Your darkest jokes?
some brand-new pure invention, notes
outside our hearing?  Or perhaps some simple tune
we'd never have made much sense of,
the one about hope.  The one about oldest love.

# Her Dying as a Bird: Small Fantasy for a Beloved Aunt

*for Mary, keeper of family history
and genealogy, manners, morals, and
fashions, dying in springtime at eighty-three*


Bunched on a near branch, breast
puffed out like a pomegranate,
Robin is twilight.
She who is usually seen runaway-stop,
runaway-stop on the family field
sits now in a final preen.
Higher, no longer sentinel of our ground,
she has other business. All inward flurry,
she's a staticky blur on her twig.

Behind her, the green of late spring
goes dim in the shade's hem beginning
its sweep, the sun still golden
one backyard over.
                    Clever robin
steals the material dark for her tail,
revising that rudder.
From silk cloak-feathers, from breast tufts
of Renaissance russet,
she expunges the dust.

Now the sky is just pearl in the oak,
now darker, now smoke. And there are no more shadows,
only the pallor of old tin.
The world tips lightly, lightly more,
unkindling sidelong until shadow's
all there is.

Now still as a leaf and finished
with bristle and flourish,

Robin looses the quick
drop of night in her eye. And gathers it back,
gathers the ragged horizon tight,
a black sack with everything in it:
the string of backyards, all of us stopped
like a family portrait, the yesterday's light,
and the long generations of spring—

for the clean vanishing.

# Living for a While
# in the Country

This far from the city, it's possible
the encircling woods will yet disclose
the fox we watch for, that rough red
comet promised by the mice and rabbits
to the sun-strafed field.
Certainly the jay's jigsaw blue will break
across this light, and the clumsy grackle
will stipple a graceful iridescence
on green April air.

With a task for our hands here
in field and wood, with the small substance
these might yield; with a hard life,
we might yet earn the vivid cloth of the world
pouring from the shuddering loom—
all that is made and unmade and made again.

Perhaps in such a tapestry, a piece of us
breaks into flight, or red stealth,
or the stutter of blood on the ground.
Even the small wind among beeches bears us.
Even the minuscule flowering
of blue-eyed grass.
Out here where we are newly
in the pattern, the pattern makes nothing
but sense, can even make sensible
the history we are; as sure a course
as the one laid down by generations of deer,
barely there yet finding a creek if you stay with it.

But we are the people of right-angled paths.
We'll return to the towers of information,
the batteries of experts, the strange-banked
rivers of pavement
where everything trembles and cannot come together,

the great cables like threads patiently pulled out
by the hand of a giant who forgot them and went away.

And no love is large enough to take them up again
where there is not even a fox's flare
to snare violence into beauty.
In a war that is not a war, a burning
city stands scaffolded with lights,
undoing after undoing.

And no homecoming.

# VALENTINE AT FIFTY

Too many times I have left you.
I grew isolate as a tide pool, stubborn,
all my broken-into houses scattered.

I missed you then, the inward-turning
curve exposed and shining, the designs
of the sea's voices all over

everything. You were patient in my silences,
though you must have been sad, beachcombing,
looking for whole animals.

This is to say a vow again beside our February sea,
bone gray as any history. *I love you.*
Useless phrase. I carry it like a thing
picked up in the dunes, some crab claw
or ancient tooth, under the shadow
of the careening gull.

Saying it, the mouth still
goes through all its phases,
whole moons opening and closing.
And in it we still hear our own blood's spiraling
sibilance like the shell's, and the horizon's
distance, red and purple siberite now whole,
now touched with paths of breakage toward the dark.

# SIPHNOS, 1987

> I have seen the sun break through
> to illuminate a small field for
> awhile, and gone my way and
> forgotten it. But that was the pearl
> of great price, the one field that
> had the treasure in it.
> —R. S. Thomas, "The Bright Field"


Just past our neighbors' lemon trees
heavy with their eggs of light,
one plot of ground was measured out
by stone walls whitewashed to shining—
something I might glance toward, walking on.
It was as blunt as any field in Wales,
as full of weather in a place where weather
likewise mints the farmer's coin.
But this piece of land was given over.

I'd never seen wild flowers in such riot:
empurpled, gilded, smeared with the blue of icons.
And wide-faced poppies crowded luminous
as figures in the stained glass of cathedrals,
the blood of saints in them.
I hadn't guessed Greek sunlight could repeat
at certain moments everything
that's been said about it—*molten
gold, honey, wine*—pouring overmuch
on April's prism, making rich
even the wooden donkey saddle waiting
daisy-bestridden, beneath an almond tree.

In air so clear, any sound will carry
until it seems almost material
beneath a sky that holds its clarity
the way St. Spirodon's blue dome
above the dark chants holds perfection.
A fisherman in the village square was calling

the names of his catch, red mullet
leaping in his voice. The priest's donkey
clattered past in a stutter of yellow.
Behind the stone church, a woman
in a moan of black skirts combed
her child's hair softly with a song
green as the turning sea.
And surely the ragged wail sent down
by the goat lost on the mountain
bore the violet bruises of despair.

I stayed the morning there, in thrall
to something in particular.
Memory has taken it: white wall, the shine
of voices, the blossoms plying like gaudy fish
their sea of wind.
This was the bright field, the burning bush
that startles stone to words. It outstays
Mycenae's gate, Delphi's high and sibilant ruin;
the laws already broken
of matter and of time.

# THE BIRD WOMAN

*for Barbara Johnson*


She takes them as they come
from the hands of strangers, in shoeboxes and paper cups,
wrapped in handkerchiefs, in Kmart cages.

She splints the hawk's wing, sews the cat-wrung
body of the wren, and feeds with an eyedropper
the wind-tossed or too zealous, fallen young.

Barefoot, small-boned—there should be words
to lift her into air the way a saint
might travel.  Or an angel.  That's not right:

whatever's hers is earthen, bought with earth,
a solitude she has not had to choose,
the break that will not fuse.

In one tall cage beside her dingy house,
two barred owls bob and whistle for their mouse.
Nearby, a lone black skimmer limps and cries.

What keeps the healer company in sleep?
A crooked wing, or blood-drops folded secret
in the cardinal's scarlet cloak?
Perhaps she dreams the hollow featherless bone,
at last perfected, has become her own
extended shoulder, feels the dove's sad tripled note
stir like a nest of fledglings in her throat.

Daily she wakes to this world, daily
holds the wings of death at bay,
though otherworldly colors lean
into the harpstrings of her backyard's light:
the kestrel with a sunrise on his back,

the jay's noon blue, the warbler's hood of gold.
And the nightjar's twilight-shaded sweep,
the startled grackle's black rainbow.

Bits of heaven's weather, pieces of the sky
fall here. And by the ground this woman keeps,
they rise. They rise.

III

# In a Trunk Not Looked into for Twenty Years

Snapshots curled in rigor mortis,
cuff links with the emblems of a lodge,
braided hair rings, a whistle, marbles,
hodgepodge of pocket knives, tin tops . . .
and here, Father, is that ringbox
I'd forgotten—in your faded
handwriting three words: *Redbud. Dark red.*

The box holds two small seeds
shining like brown taffeta.

Here in my hand is your shy love for color.
The painter you might have been spoke once
when you told us all the story of the doll
you saw as a boy at a carnival—
how you loved her dress of scarlet silk,
how it shown still on barbs of memory.
You were thirteen, a crack shot.
And you won. No one laughed
at the uneasy prize you chose:
to hold that bright material awhile
before your delighted sisters got the doll.

Flowers you'd bring from hunting trips
would be as dead before you got them home
as any meat you'd shot—
wild orchids we didn't know were rare,
carnivorous sundew, bluebonnets
too blue, bogflowers nameless and scarce.
Sometimes you'd have a branch of redbud
wilting beside you in the truck.
You said it kept the winter back.

*Dark red.* You'd found a strange one,
deeper colored, extraordinary. You marked the place
and you came back in autumn for the seeds.
You thought I'd want to raise
in my suburban backyard a thing uncanny
as your wilderness kept turning out to be,
where creek banks sown with the teeth of ancient seas
bloomed with furred and pliant shadows,
where the green air turned and turned
its whirligig of birds.

When I was a child, you sketched them all for me,
each creature in its chosen place,
even the serpent curled on a branch, asleep.
I have the pencil drawings still,
bleached but full of detail, primitive
and skilled and wary as the animals themselves
printing their tracks on that preyed-over ground.

Now I've just returned from another country—
the whole Peloponnese was snared in bloom.
At Olympia, the broken columns lay
in a shoal of Judas trees,
the hold of Zeus ashimmer in pink fire.
Redbud. Judas tree. The same
branches of such ill luck they had to bear
the awful dead weight of remorse.
Greek blossoms surged like fountains
among the shattered temples, betrayal everywhere.

I've heard of seeds taken from a tomb
in Egypt, planted in sterile soil, and brought to bloom.
Not here, Father. Nothing's here
but this inheritance: my imagining eye
sketching on a windowpane the strange
vision of a tree like a scarlet skirt
afire among ghosts of the shrinking forest,
suddenly bright
as the spreading blossom of blood you lost,
and desperate with spring.

# At the Age When You Get Bad News

Letting go of the future
is like this: trying to fit
back into the camera's aperture
before it closed that little square of time.
In this snapshot, I am fifteen,
all opening before me. I squint hard
against such brightness; perhaps I feared
the shutter's snicker.

Memory adds to what's outside the frame—
that fence, all rough-barked wood,
where my grandfather hung the dead
rattlesnake that wouldn't stay dead.
That fence, and the field beyond it
overgrown, one slightly agitated cow
heading for a shade tree.

But all that's beyond the picture's reach.
Here I am, feckless and posing.
My father stands beside me with his stick.
He's looking down so there's no face to him,
just hat with the brim turned down.
I'm wearing the sweater of pale lavender
that seemed made for someone prettier,
like the deep purple skirt
of corduroy soft as velvet.
It's all gray in this black–and–white,
the colors I'll get where I'm going.

In the picture I'm sitting on my heels
hugging the cur named Red
my father kept for squirrels,
and some of those in the out-of-focus trees
making the big dog's head begin its easy
swing toward joy, just as I am turning already
toward the path to this day two thousand miles away

that has brought me another death
and this kind of travel—
I do manage to get there before the picture,
where it's darker than it ever gets
until you've traveled afterward yourself.
Nobody's looked yet through the finder,
the lens not set, boundaries of white
paper not yet interrupting a translated sun.
I don't know what's going to happen
all over again at the speed of light:
the trees, my father, the blank sweater,
that dog starting to run.

# Time at the Movies

Say we move through our days some way secure
in other people's moments,
each one of us a star in several reels
of the lives of any number of our friends,
our relatives, our enemies.
We're parts—sometimes walk-ons, sometimes leads—
in separate plays that replay in the minds
of those we know
know us.

That party where the drunk blew up
and you were heroic.  Or useless.  What you were.
And the awful night that love affair left off,
when you were absurd, or reasonable, or cruel.
And on that toppled birthday, didn't the wrong
present tumble from the box?
Then once, for reasons you've forgotten,
you made your father cry.

Someone remembers.  If not as you remember,
at least in the neighborhood,
though circumstance and outcome may be changed,
and the color of your hair and what you said.
Never mind how various and unstrung
the world: it still is *you*
in that mind's eye, flickering.

Imagine all of us together in one place,
each person holding strands that reach to *then*
and you in it: eighth grade, the summer after college,
the year you had that dog that may have been
all black, or white with brown spots.
And you hold lines to all the other pasts,
the people in them.

They in your life and you in theirs are like
a city full of lights one sees by
whether there's a moon or not.
Or like lights crossing underwater, unmistakable
but wavering so you cannot see the source.
And with it all a kind of music, voices
dissonant, disarranged as dream. We move
by what you could call keeping time.
And now and then a tug on some taut line
can bring you up still gasping and still you.

Now imagine, little by little
the skeins of light, the sounds crisscrossing,
start to scatter and to dim
the way a house will darken bit by bit
as one by one the people there turn in
to dreamless sleep, talk fallen into quiet.
But you, stalled wherever you are, stay sure
of conversation and entanglement,
of bright beams trolling the dark,
though the pantomime
goes fast to shadow or to snow.

Until you sense the blank the world's become
and you forget yourself.
And they are gone.

# Written at a Country Mansion of the 1920s, Now Partially Restored as a Writing Retreat for Poets

Our shoes clamor in empty chambers,
room after room, where the sunlight's
asleep on bare floors.
Beyond the french doors, the gardens crouch
deranged beneath their wild invaders.
Only high pines and willows
have kept their places. The hollows
of the vast house whine with carpentry,
dust rising to spangle a column
of sun haunting the staircase.

It is impossible not to imagine the past here,
its clichés of pleasure: how the articulate
guests dropped their shoes on Aubussons
in the quiet hour, dressing for dinner
those evenings that arrived in their best,
their ice-clear stars.
Horses sighed in the stables,
water in the pool, flame on the candles.

As if things were simple.

For you who raised this house, I cast
a time more yellow with summer than ours,
an ease even you could not have known you owned.
And I give you power's inevitable daydream:
a pause, say after luncheon when murmurs

of servants diminished, when the guests
had gone each to his right train.
I place you in the wedge of sun
that broke across a polished table edge
when it came—the sudden bad moment
like a weather of stone—and you thought
of your heart while the air raced with invisible
wheels, and something like war seemed to pull
at the garden, something like death, something worse
in a flood of unfurnishing light.
Might the word *thieves* have drifted on your lips,
a wish to refurbish the locks, a whisper
directed to no one?

Before you could blink away erasure, before
you could wake wholly to the afternoon's
cut flowers, the mirrors, the folded headlines
from Europe, a hand across your eyes—
you might have guessed, almost,
the longleaf pines around this house
the last of their thousand mile forest,
light changing into *future,* the workings of light
become knowledge toward annihilation.
And you might have seen us, strangers flickering
dark here, darker. And the whippoorwill
practicing a dying art.

# New South

It's lovely where we live. We chose it
maybe because there aren't grapevines or blackberries.
This neighborhood is all those natural-seeming
yards that cost so much to keep them seeming
natural. The city's nice enough. And far enough away.
Sometimes I remember there are no graveyards here,
no stone angels standing on the dead,
ready to take to the air but staying.
Nobody seems to *be* dead. Where are they?
If they were ever here it isn't mentioned.

The friends I've made are smart and talented.
And I know them all so well I might imagine
they are myself. Almost. There's a prickly quick
energy in them, a kind of light. I borrow that.
I borrow. Lately some of them have borrowed back:
they're buying antique quilts to stretch and hang
like paintings on their walls. And something in that
shocks me—scraps of nameless lives hung up,
not warming anything in those white rooms.
So like my white rooms, so why should it feel strange?

I have a dozen quilts myself, all marked
with the names and dates of ancestors who made them,
and folded in a chest as old as they are.
How blame my friends for buying what I thought
you had to have already, make, or never have?
Or for hanging quilts like art instead of keeping
use alive? I guess it's part of the whole past
it was so terribly important that we lose.
And then enclose to look at in museums.
Still, I like a horizontal seeing,

looking at history. My quilts stay what you might call
*active*—it reminds me of the time I volunteered
with the Elder Center out near Holly Springs.
Those country women quilted every Thursday,

and the social worker who runs the place told me:
*It's sad. They could sell these quilts so easily*
*if they didn't use those polyester pieces*
*and ruin the authenticity.* I told her then
that you use for quilts whatever the life has used,
and if that's some of polyester then it's right.

Because isn't that what being authentic is?
I could get mixed up between *preservation*
and *nostalgia* tacky as polyester. I know
the past's not real. And never was, somebody said.
You can hang it up one way (like Williamsburg)
as what you want. Or hang it another way
as what you fear. Either one will change it.
Once I saw Native Australian sand paintings
reduced to manageable size, made permanent
with glue on canvas so we could take them in.

And they were fine to see, but they'd given up
the ritual that lived in their huge temporary form:
the ground itself, even wind that had to scatter
the pattern, all lived as part of the necessity
of making. Lately I've not been quite sure
what ground I'm standing on. As if I'd waked
in Belgium after starting out for Beaumont—
and with this hurtful worry, a kind of sickness
for things changed or missing, things that pass,
the air around me thick and still. Like glass.

# A DEATH

Our aged cat has sickened. We did make
the right decision—the gentle veterinarian
says we did. Now I'm allowed to hold him
wrapped in a blue towel against the cold
of the metal table. He lies in my arms
and purrs as he would at home, secure
while death crawls along a vein,
then skids into his eyes. They stop,
alarmed, then fixed, then not.

Just a cat. But all of life is just
one or another. And each one
may live so much, so far. And must.
The world's not just.
A natural end for him would be
only narrow and deeply cruel—
as we secretly feel ourselves to be,
taking him home in a box.
                              How naturally
even kindness runs
the same round course as everything:
a planet, not a sun.

# WRITING POEMS LATE

The summer's little clocks, soft works awhir,
are loose among the darkening trees, weighting the air
exactly as they did that year when death
turned suddenly original—

and here I stop
as surely as a summer's voices thin
to sere and silence in the closing hand of cold.
Already it is a kind of winter, this ice on the tongue.
If I were a bird, I'd be the wrong one. A toad
is more appropriate for any ode we'd have:
it sleeps and waits
to make its ugly revolution in
the glass-jar air of what we'll take for spring.

If I speak of a porch light that still casts,
somewhere, that peculiar deepened yellow glow
you'd seen on summer nights against the leaning house?
That's only sepia the memory layers over
what will print but cannot last,
like shadow in its clockwise march.
The scene I won't flesh into words could make me weep—

and that is disallowed, of course, unless
for grief addressable, a present tense
quite shadowless and pure:
*The World as System* or *Language as a City*—
the critics, agile as paramecia, play
under a sun renewed, always renewed—
*The Ideological Gesture, Historical Overdetermination,*
*The Absence of a Transcendental Signified,*
and *Authenticity, Meditations on.*

Meantime there is this old demanding
repetition: memory thick as evening in the trees,

the pool of yellow porchlight full of wings
beyond which the first real dark has come
in a metallic skirl, a din
as of icebergs touching in another world.

# ILLUMINATIONS

I don't know when he died. When we were children,
we thought he must be older than the river.
The flesh on his long bones had gone
from black to gray, as if inside him
some drowned lamp was rising.

Every afternoon he cut the lawns,
sometimes with a scythe, a thing
we had no name for yet.
And no one spoke his name to us.
Everywhere he went he took the crooked
but oddly graceful walking cane he'd made
of burnt-out flashlights soldered end to end
and finished with a piece of tapered wood.

In town he tapped it hard, as if for attention,
for something he might be about to say.
And when he worked the yards, it shone
out of the grass where he'd laid it down
like Aaron's rod or some magician's
silver wand, its bright red buttons
lined up straight, its thumbed shiny switches.

Of course we made up what might happen if
he ever played that instrument,
what might glow or be snapped off,
and whether good or bad would leap
in the power we thought it kept.

And when he'd disappear for weeks or months,
we made up matchless reasons for his going.
We gave him the richest thing we had: our fear
of all real mystery. We had so much to figure out
of what went on around us in the dark,
it was what we knew best: not knowing.

Those last years, he gave up work—even the churchyard—
and took to walking every hot dirt road
in the whole county, and every street around
the courthouse square, his stick still gleaming,
tapping and raising dust.
We'd follow sometimes, at a distance, quiet.

I believe we thought he'd turn to us and tell it,
whatever it was.  Or turn on us with it.
Then at least we'd either know, or have to run—
we had a question but we didn't know what question.
Of course he never even turned.
Did we?
        I can't remember when we lost him,
when we forgot
            to look for him in riddles of our own.

It would be years before we'd see the light.

# EAST TEXAS AUTUMN
## AS A WAY TO SEE TIME

After the coded messages of wild geese are over,
misinterpreted as merely weather,
and after a few sharp nights have dipped
starpoint by starpoint to unstitch
the green from the meadows—
                                        but before
the first chainlinks of ice have shut
the wings of twilight fiddlers and the gate
of the spider's vacant wheelhouse—
                                        here's November
again, turned hot and sucking a groundfog.

It bears the bodies of my people, all given
to disappearing so suddenly in this season,
the dirt had them before the wind could change.
By poisoned blood, locked heart, bad lungs, by bullet,
they were plunged deep where the year darkened
just *here*.
            As if there were a rule about it.

I've been gone so long I had forgotten
how a docile chill will just graze
the edges of morning and evening
holding between them a pillowful
of bright feathers, a trembling
of the thinnest wishbones passing tuneful
through this country, disassembling overhead
another summer.
                    I could misremember
where the anniversaries are,
now that the downed, quilt-bright
leaves are soft underfoot,
though the trees are still ringing with color.

Here the ground lets the wet go,
suspiration of old rain climbing
visibly skyward in fog-rags.

                    A cold breath intaken.

By noon, alarum of sumac, boom
of red oak and maple, the ample light
cracking its whip, the holler of yellow
ditch-flowers, and every elbowing creek
a tributary to the old story of long lost
who never will come home—
down to the last chirper under
a dead bitterweed:

            *never, never.*
It might as well be military,
the nights speaking skeletal sermons
windy as any general's.

               And now,
now is the falling
forgetful under the last spell of lowland heat
turning over its brass to the brown earth victor.

Guessed at in the vaporous, piney margins,
the fugitive, brave impostor,
the season caught out of uniform,
caught out as a girl,
a girl, a dancer captured
in her own sweet turn. Almost
this minute she is quickest, loud-lit
with the cymbals of sundown—but not quite
yet and not for long and not likely
to leave more than a tatter of crimson
costume on the barbed-wire fence that is vanishing
over the softened hills, the little valleys
whose cattle are up to their knees in mist,
the still warm, silvered breath of this world
not quite undone.

Squint awhile. The distant fenceposts seem to move, become
a line of stragglers lost out of battle and gone
west, oh west, to tell

over the one campfire and ashes of dawn
November's tale: the bell in the blood,
the bright maps of birds, the world unhooded
in gunmetal light.
     How nobody won.

# VERSO

I

Walking the deepening back pasture,
I'd let pine copse and barn
fall into dusk, let the cows blur
against the herding dark,
before I'd look west to the small rise
laden with sunset.  Everything, even my breath,
my small steps whispering in grass,
grew large and important in that shadow.
I walked cloaked in the precarious songs
of late summer, katydid and creek frog.
And when I did turn, there would be,
where I knew it would be,
the great dead oak on its reddening hillock.

It stood like something commemorative,
a tall stammer of substance not taken in,
wearing all the directions of growth
but seasonless, colorless, hard
as a language I hadn't heard but must answer.
The tree had stood its own thorough wind
for as long as I could remember.
All that summer I came there at evening,
bearing invisible grief like an offering,
the big hill behind me receding
until the house with its careful garden
went out like an empty lamp.

For the tree I imagined a summer
*not here,* a green crown underground, and a red
autumn there in its time.  I imagined
this visible height was the stretch
of bare roots into air.
If the dead were nourished by heaven,
wouldn't it be so? and the bloom

underground their eternity?
*Here* still though hidden beneath
their carved names.
Who knows why a child makes a picture
then fits the world to it? The wild conjecture
I promised a hillside was surrogate
temple, monolith, loss incarnate.


2

Late, from my upper-floor window
I could see, bright night or moonless,
the branched form that leached from the far
lights of town the means of its outline.
It glowed pale as a watch dial, angled
like a walker into a gale.

And after I'd cried my mother to sleep
under her roof of earth, under her stone
star, absence fell with me to dreaming—
the ceiling, floor, doorframe all one
plane: then bright birds flew from beneath
my eyelids, from my fingertips, from my hair
to circle the branching river run upward
out in the yard, to perch on the mimicked
vein-tree of the body, maps of the palm,
a taperless candelabrum magicked
with wings of recision, with praise.


3

Of course the tree finally came down
years past my fantasy or notice.
Its wood filled the fireplaces

of three or four houses around.
But even here, a thousand miles from my childhood;
even now, my love, as you walk
across our suburban lawn toward this house
that hardly ever vanishes; even now
as you move through the smoke of first dark,
the birds in my wrists begin stirring,
knowing we're dying, knowing we shine
like that shining, all bone, all bone.